When You Were
Very Small

To

Baby Schultz

From

Tiffany, Aliah, Amanda,
ERICA & Neva
CLARKE

For Jenna K.S

WHEN YOU WERE VERY SMALL
Copyright © 2006 by Good Books, Intercourse, PA 17534
This 8" x 8" paperback was first published in 2006.
International Standard Book Number: 978-1-56148-554-3
Library of Congress Catalog Card Number: 2005024733

Text by Sophie Piper
Illustrations copyright © 2005 Kristina Stephenson

Original edition published in English under the title *On the Day You Were Born*
by Lion Hudson plc, Oxford, England. Copyright © Lion Hudson 2005

North American edition entitled **When You Were Very Small**
published by Good Books, 2006

Printed and bound in China.

Library of Congress Cataloging-in-Publication Data

Piper, Sophie.
  When you were very small / Sophie Piper Kristina Stephenson.
    p. cm.
  Summary: A parent relates how special and loved a child has been through all of the
growth and changes that have occurred since the day of its birth.
  ISBN 1-56148-554-3 (paperback)
  [1. Babies--Fiction. 2. Parent and child--Fiction.] I. Stephenson,
Kristina, ill. II. Title.
  PZ7.P6375Whe 2006
  [E]--dc22   2005024733

When You Were Very Small

Sophie Piper  Kristina Stephenson

Good ❀ Books

Intercourse, PA 17534
800/762-7171
www.GoodBooks.com

On the day you were born
you were very small,
very special,

and very clever.

From your first day, you could do lots of things:

breathing and
sleeping,

waking and
looking.

You taught us all to understand your little noises. Whatever did you want?

More food? More sleep? Dry clothes? A big hug? What a good game that was!

You taught us all to be kind and gentle.

When you fell asleep on our laps, we would sit still for ages.

Very quickly, you began to grow up. You learned to sit and smile. No one has a smile quite like yours.

You learned to talk

and to walk.

You learned to climb

and to run.

What an adventurer
you are now!

Every day, you are learning how to do new things all by yourself:

dressing,

playing with friends,

looking at books.

You're even beginning to think of what you might be when you grow up:

a builder,

a painter,

a doctor.

There are so many
things you can
dream of
being:

an explorer,

a pet-shop-
keeper,

a dancer.

Forever and for always,
you are a very special
person.

Forever and for always,
I will love you, as I have
always loved you since
the day you were born.